SERMON OF SUSTAINABILITY

Abhijit Naskar is the twenty-first century Neuroscientist whose contributions in Cognitive and Behavioral Neuroscience have helped the world tackle the issues of systemic racism, prejudice, hate, extremism, discrimination and biases more effectively. As an untiring advocate of mental health and universal acceptance, he became a beloved best-selling author all over the world with his very first book "The Art of Neuroscience in Everything". With his pioneering ventures into the Neuropsychology of beliefs and biases, he has hugely contributed in the eradication of religious and cultural differences in our world, for which he is popularly hailed as the humanitarian scientist, who takes the human civilization in the path of sweet general harmony.

Find A Cause
Outside Yourself
Sermon of Sustainability

ABHIJIT NASKAR

Find A Cause Outside Yourself: Sermon of Sustainability

An Amazon Publishing Company, 1st Edition, 2022

Printed in the United States of America

ISBN: 9798838739872

Also by Abhijit Naskar

The Art of Neuroscience in Everything
Your Own Neuron: A Tour of Your Psychic Brain
The God Parasite: Revelation of Neuroscience
The Spirituality Engine
Love Sutra: The Neuroscientific Manual of Love
Homo: A Brief History of Consciousness
Neurosutra: The Abhijit Naskar Collection
Autobiography of God: Biopsy of A Cognitive Reality
Biopsy of Religions: Neuroanalysis towards Universal
Tolerance
Prescription: Treating India's Soul
What is Mind?
In Search of Divinity: Journey to The Kingdom of Conscience
Love, God & Neurons: Memoir of a scientist who found
himself by getting lost
The Islamophobic Civilization: Voyage of Acceptance
Neurons of Jesus: Mind of A Teacher, Spouse & Thinker
Neurons, Oxygen & Nanak
The Education Decree
Principia Humanitas
The Krishna Cancer
Rowdy Buddha: The First Sapiens
We Are All Black: A Treatise on Racism
The Bengal Tigress: A Treatise on Gender Equality
Either Civilized or Phobic: A Treatise on Homosexuality
Wise Mating: A Treatise on Monogamy
Illusion of Religion: A Treatise on Religious
Fundamentalism
The Film Testament
Human Making is Our Mission: A Treatise on Parenting
I Am The Thread: My Mission
7 Billion Gods: Humans Above All
Lord is My Sheep: Gospel of Human
Morality Absolute
A Push in Perception
Let The Poor Be Your God
Conscience over Nonsense
Saint of The Sapiens
Time to Save Medicine
Fabric of Humanity
Build Bridges not Walls: In the name of Americana
The Constitution of The United Peoples of Earth

Lives to Serve Before I Sleep
When Humans Unite: Making A World Without Borders
All For Acceptance
Monk Meets World
Mission Reality
Citizens of Peace: Beyond The Savagery of Sovereignty
Operation Justice: To Make A Society That Needs No Law
See No Gender
The Gospel of Technology
Every Generation Needs Caretakers: The Gospel of
Patriotism
Aşkanjali: The Sufi Sermon
Mad About Humans: World Maker's Almanac
Revolution Indomable
When Call The People: My World My Responsibility
No Foreigner Only Family
Hurricane Humans: Give me accountability, I'll give you
peace
Ain't Enough to Look Human
Servitude is Sanctitude
Time To End Democracy: The Meritocratic Manifesto
I Vicdansaadet Speaking: No Rest Till The World is Lifted
Boldly Comes Justice: Sentient not Silent
Good Scientist: When Science and Service Combine
Sleepless for Society
Neden Türk: The Gospel of Secularism
Martyr Meets World: To Solve The Hard Problem of
Inhumanity
The Shape of A Human: Our America Their America
When Veins Ignite: Either Integration or Degradation
Heart Force One: Need No Gun to Defend Society
Solo Standing on Guard: Life Before Law
Generation Corazon: Nationalism is Terrorism
Mucize Insan: When The World is Family
Hometown Human: To Live for Soil and Society
Girl Over God: The Novel (Abi Naskar Adventures Book 1)
Gente Mente Adelante: Prejudice Conquered is World
Conquered
Earthquakin' Egalitarian: I Die Everyday So Your Children
Can Live
Giants in Jeans: 100 Sonnets of United Earth
Vatican Virus: The Forbidden Fiction (Abi Naskar
Adventures Book 2)
Karadeniz Chronicle: The Novel (Abi Naskar Adventures

Book 3)
Şehit Sevda Society: Even in Death I Shall Live
Handcrafted Humanity: 100 Sonnets For A Blunderful
World
Mücadele Muhabbet: Gospel of An Unarmed Soldier
Making Britain Civilized: How to Gain Readmission to The
Human Race
Dervish Advaitam: Gospel of Sacred Feminines and Holy
Fathers
Honor He Wrote: 100 Sonnets For Humans Not Vegetables
The Gentalist: There's No Social Work, Only Family Work
Either Reformist or Terrorist: If You Are Terror I Am Your
Grandfather
Woman Over World: The Novel (Abi Naskar Adventures
Book 4)
High Voltage Habib: Gospel of Undoctrination
Bulldozer on Duty

*This book is dedicated to those who know the
difference between necessity and luxury.*

CONTENTS

1.   Welcome To Earth (World Tourism Sonnet)....1

2.   The Best Luxury 5

3.   Health and Sickness (The Sonnet) 9

4.   Medicine Means (The Sonnet) 13

5.   A Life Realized 17

6.   Never Planned (The Sonnet) 21

7.   Tapwater and Natural Spring (The Sonnet)...25

8.   Self Outside The Self 29

9.   Myth of Sustainability 33

10.   Simplicity Over Celebrity 39

11.   Are You Alive 45

12.   There is No Sustainability Problem 49

13.   Love, Latitude, Longitude (The Sonnet)....53

14.   Ruined Lover (The Sonnet) 57

15.   Beyond Recognition 61

16.   No Collaboration With Cancer 65

17.   Money Doesn't Fix The World................69

18.   One Sense Above All........................73

19.   Scrutiny Must Never Cease 79

20.   Old and New (The Sonnet) 85

21.   Fortune Without Love (The Sonnet) 89

22.   It Won't Be Easy 93

23.   Sapient or Savage (The Sonnet)..............97

24.   Life is Chaos (The Sonnet).......................101

25.   Light Impossible (The Sonnet) 105

26.   Competition Breeds Sickness.................109

27.   Hate Not The Hater (The Sonnet)...........115

28.   Valley of Light (The Sonnet)...................119

29.   Be The Precedent....................................123

30.   We Are Nature's Wonder 127

31.   Peygamber   Undercover   (Sonnet   of
Accountability) 131

32.   Yeni Peygamber (Sorumluluk Şiiri – Turkish)
135

33.   Sanity and Insanity................................139

34.   People Vs Supreme Court (The Sonnet) ..143

35.   Humanity Means....................................147

BIBLIOGRAPHY 151

1.   Welcome To Earth
(World Tourism Sonnet)

ABHIJIT NASKAR

Welcome to Earth
(World Tourism Sonnet)

When you are down with doubts sit down,
For lessons of revolution from the Americas.
When you are beginning to have cold feet,
Siphon some much needed resilience from Africa.
When your heart is beginning to turn cold,
Have a rejuvenating swim in the warmth of Asia.
When clouds of gloom start to grab hold,
Breathe in some fresh air from Australia.
Whenever the bickering goes overboard,
Draw some lessons of unity from Europe.
Whatever it is you seek my friend,
We just might be able to satisfy your hope.
Come visit us sometime, on our little blue dot.
We are the beings of love, light and colors,
as such we often go overboard.

2. The Best Luxury

The best luxury is least luxury. Den bästa lyxen är minst lyxen. This is the scandi way. This is the foundation of nordic life - nay, this is the foundation of healthy, whole, undistracted human life. Call it lagom, call it mys, call it hygge - it all comes down to one simple fact - health, happiness and sustainability come not through over-abundance or scarcity, but through balance - through moderation - through self-regulation.

Some intellectuals may argue, don't mys and hygge mean indulgence! To which I say, here indulgence doesn't mean going all out in a big and fancy way, it means indulging in little things - simple things. In short, health and happiness come through indulging in simple things - through simplicity.

Sustainability lies in simplicity. A simple life is a healthy life. Happiness happens not by avoiding pain, but by avoiding luxury – by avoiding materialistic obsession. The more obsessed we are with materials, with possessions, the more miserable we'll be.

So, first and foremost, shift your focus from materials to mind - from possession to people -

and all the necessary happiness will come chasing after you.

Let me put this into perspective. Good food doesn't mean fancy food, good friend doesn't mean fancy friend, good life doesn't mean fancy life.

You see, despite the fact that this materialistic world confuses good with fancy, fancy and good are actually antithesis of each other. As a matter of fact, what is fancy often ends up being unhealthy, and rather lethal, for the individual as well as the society.

3. Health and Sickness
(The Sonnet)

10

Health and Sickness
(The Sonnet)

Health doesn't always come from pills,
Health comes through being mindful.
Pills just help bring down the barriers,
That clutter the body with deadly ghoul.
Wellness is not the absence of sickness,
It's the capacity to overcome sickness.
Some sickness are the norm of nature,
Others are products of our own foolishness.
The opposite of sickness is not its absence,
The opposite of sickness is its awareness.
To treat sickness we must first acknowledge it,
Sickness acknowledged is sickness half treated.
In the end, health favors those who favor humility.
Sustainability favors those who favor simplicity.

4. Medicine Means
(The Sonnet)

14

Medicine Means
(The Sonnet)

MEDICINE means Mercy,
MEDICINE means Empathy,
MEDICINE means Dare,
MEDICINE means Integrity,
MEDICINE means Care,
MEDICINE means Ingenuity,
MEDICINE means Nobility,
MEDICINE means Ethicality.
Medicine is not a profession,
Medicine is but a sacred calling.
An average doctor saves a body,
A good doctor saves a being.
Pathogens exist to cash in on sickness.
A doctor exists to be lost among patients.

16

5. A Life Realized

As I said, sustainability comes through simplicity, which means that we gotta wipe out every last trace of fanciness from our life. We gotta move from the pursuit of luxury to the pursuit of simplicity.

But then again, when we talk about simplicity, there is really nothing to pursue, for simplicity is the realization of life itself. Once life is realized, that is the end of all pursuit, and the beginning of the ultimate exploration – the exploration of ourselves – the exploration of our potential – the exploration of the humanity within the humans. And this, my friend, is the true final frontier.

There is really nothing simpler than sustainability. We just gotta uncomplicate our life. We have to return to a simpler way of living, while redirecting our drive for advancement in places that really matter.

By returning to a simpler of way of living, I don't mean returning to the caves, rather what I am asking of you is this.

Instead of saturating life with more comfort, we gotta focus on equalizing life. For example, I never wanted to be famous. All I ever wanted was to lift up the world, that is, to equalize the world. Besides, whom would I be famous for - a bunch of materialistic snobs!

Fame and reform do not go together. Fame and reformer do not go together.

Let me tell you a secret. You shall never find a reformer where there is fame. You shall never find a reformer in the lap of luxury. To put it simply, fame repels the reformer, luxury repels the reformer.

Or perhaps I should say, reformer repels luxury, for where there is luxury, there is no life - where there is life, there can be no luxury. That's why you'll find a reformer in the dust of the street and the dirt of the soil, not in a large mansion surrounded by fancy cars and empty yesmen.

I'll say it to you plainly. Luxury is the antithesis of life. Therefore, luxury is the antithesis of sustainability.

To build a sustainable world is quite easy, what apparently is not easy is to get rid of our self-absorption. Give up the pursuit of luxury, and sustainability will pour out of your veins.

6. Never Planned
    (The Sonnet)

22

Never Planned
(The Sonnet)

I never planned to be a poet,
I never planned to be a writer.
I never planned to be a scientist,
I never planned to be a philosopher.
I never had any plans whatsoever,
As to what I was going to be.
As a vagabond I only had one inkling,
That is to equalize the society.
Now that I am a scientist,
Logic comes to me like clockwork.
Now that I am a writer and poet,
Words and rhymes come like lovewalk.
The path appears itself as you start to walk.
Means flow like heartbeat in all purposeful work.

7. Tapwater and Natural Spring
(The Sonnet)

26

Tapwater and Natural Spring
(The Sonnet)

I am sorry if big bard becomes bleak,
In front of the vast spirit of oneness.
I am sorry if baron byron turns barren,
In front of the sense of collectiveness.
With their native tongue given at birth,
The fancy figures did what they could.
It ain't their fault that it takes an outsider,
To bring out a tongue's rightful good.
Some figures are tapwater,
While others are natural spring.
Some are just good writers,
While others are Maya, Martí and King.
Anybody can write mushy words, that's no biggie.
Genius is one who lives as they speak, with integrity.

8.   Self Outside The Self

To do any good to the world, first you gotta find a cause outside yourself. Those who can look beyond the needs of the self are the very vessels of sustainability - they are the very source of sustainability.

Remember the three S - Society, Sustainability, Simplicity. This is the key to a healthy, harmonious and progressive civilization.

Sustainability is simple, but it will remain ever so complex, so long as we are run by selfishness. Sustainability is simplicity in practice, sustainability is unselfishness in practice.

But then again, what is unselfishness?

Is it the absence of the self?

Self-absorbed snobs may perceive the terms "unselfishness" and "selflessness" to be the absence of the self, but in reality, it is anything but that.

Unselfishness or selflessness is not the absence of the self, it is the absence of an exclusive self, and the presence of an inclusive self - the presence of an expansive self – a self without barriers, a self without sects, a self outside the self.

Hence, sustainability doesn't mean limiting yourself, it means liberating yourself from the prehistoric chains of divisionism and from the modern chains of materialism.

It is this simple. We need materials to live, but if we think of materials to be life itself, then that's it - we are dead already - so is all possibility of sustainability - so is all possibility of health, harmony and humanity.

So I say again, find a cause outside yourself, and all will be sustainable. Find the self outside the self, and all will be harmonious.

And instead of focusing on fancy philosophical terms like sustainability and harmony, why not simply focus on simplicity - why not just focus on simple living!

9. Myth of Sustainability

Where there is simplicity, there is sustainability. Där det finns enkelhet finns det hållbarhet. Donde hay simplicidad, hay sostenabilidad.

When there is simplicity in our life, there will sustainability in the world. A materialistic and self-absorbed world chasing after the so-called sustainable development goals is like a super-obese dog chasing after its own tail.

Let me elaborate.

In a self-absorbed world sustainability is a myth. In a simple and gentle world sustainability is the norm. So let's forget about sustainability. Let's forget about sustainable development goals. These are all gimmick. I'll tell you why.

Sustainable development goals is actually the privileged lot's code for 'let's screw this world with our narcissistic shenanigans, then we can make TV shows on us pretending to fix the world's problems that we continue to create with our lavish, self-centric lifestyle.'

It's not a global goal, it's a global scam, sold by the rich to the rich at the expense of everybody else - at the expense of the working people of planet earth.

I wonder. Am I being too harsh?

Perhaps I am, but then again, as I tend to scrutinize my radical statement like I always do, it dawned on me just now that, this planet has never been the home of the human race, it has always been the home of the rich and privileged, while the rest of humanity slave their butt off, barely scraping by on hand-me-downs and leftovers.

The privileged screw the world, then the privileged pretend to fix the world. What a joke!

I have said this before, and I'll repeat once again. I am not against the United Nations and all their fantabulous initiatives, heck, I would be pleased to work with them (not for them) if they ever ask me. But let me make one thing absolutely clear. No institution is above the people, not the White House, not the Kremlin, not the White Hall, and not the United Nations either.

So instead of focusing on intellectual pomposities like sustainable development goals, the next time you indulge in a luxury, ask yourself, is it a luxury you really need – if not, how many lives you could lift with the resources spent on that particular luxury!

Let me put it into perspective. One fancy apple watch could feed a family of four in the developing parts of the world for half a year.

So, stop talking about sustainable development goals, and start practicing sustainable habits.

10. Simplicity Over Celebrity

I am a brain scientist, a behaviorist, and as such it is my duty to point out the obvious potholes of primitiveness embedded deep in the neural circuits of human nature, to which even the glorious United Nations is not infallible. That is why till this day either desperately or subconsciously the UN keeps falling at the feet of celebrities to add recognition to their cause without ever looking into their character beyond their celebrity.

That in my book is called boot-licking, not world-building.

Not all movie stars are without character, but the world has a messed up habit of confusing fame with character – the world has a messed up belief that just because they are movie stars, involving their name is good for business. This very notion is what I have trouble with.

Fun fact: exceptions aside, this is the hidden agenda behind universities giving honorary doctorates to celebrities.

Hence, I have only this to say to the UN.

Stop making movie stars your ambassadors, just so you could grab a little attention from the people. Seek out the reformers from the streets and the soil, and put them in charge. Only by doing this shall you earn your rightful place under the sun, instead of just hogging up space as a celebrity-chasing junkyard.

And if you can't even face this simple fact of human nature, then I guess there is no difference between you lot and the white supremacists, who won't even let children learn about history because they fear that learning the truth will make them hate themselves.

I truly hope that you are better than them, my dear UN. Because you matter.

And just for the record - if you must make a movie star your ambassador, then find one who has no trace of lavishness or arrogance in their life and personality.

Now let's get back to the matter at hand. Let's cut the crap about sustainability. Let's forget all these phony activism, and focus simply on a simple life instead.

Let's focus on awareness over convenience. Let's focus on character over comfort. Once we do that, all things great will follow, not just for the self, but for the society, for our species.

Focus on a cause, focus on a purpose, focus on a mission, focus on an act. Choose one thing, and do it till you drop dead. That's how you sustain a world - that's how you sustain yourself - that's how you become immortal.

No matter who joins you or not, live your life as the vessel of your purpose - live your life as civilization incarnate. Live your life not as a sample of what is, but as an example of what could be.

11. Are You Alive

Let me ask you this. Are you alive?

Not, are you breathing, or eating, or mating, or partying?

I am asking you, are you alive?

You are alive only when you are responsible. And in my eyes, a responsible individual is the only United Nations this world will ever need.

You see, equality starts at home - and how does it start - by the abolition of luxury. Wipe out every trace of luxury from your life. Keep necessities and use the rest to lift up others. This, my friend, is sustainability in action, yet you are barely going to read about it in your social studies class.

You are going to read about sustainable development goals, you are going to read about international relations, you are even going to read about economic disparities, but in all those pompous study material, you'd rarely find any emphasis on the simple act of unselfishness.

In short, as social doctors you are taught everything about how to postpone the symptoms, but nothing about treating the actual disease.

And what is the disease?

Selfishness.

Mark you, biologically speaking, selfishness is absolutely natural - there's nothing pathological about it. But humanly speaking, everything about it is pathological.

However deeming selfishness as the root of all disparities is rather displeasing to us, that's why we talk about sustainability and all that nonsense. Don't we!

12. There is No Sustainability Problem

As I have said before, earth has plenty resources to suffice our need, but no planet has enough resources to suffice our greed. No planet has enough means to meet our endless pursuit of inconsequential pleasures.

So you must ask the question.

What is consequential - what is inconsequential?

But mark you, you must ask this question, not as a person, but as a reflection of your society - a conscious, conscientious and courageous reflection of the society - of the world.

Where there is reflection, there is realization. Where there is realization, there is responsibility. Where there is responsibility, there is reformation.

There never was a sustainability problem, there is only a self-centricity problem.

Realize your responsibility towards the collective - and I mean truly, genuinely, actually – realize it to your very core - and all self-centricity will lose their power over you.

No institution can outweigh the valor and virtue of the individual. And to be specific, by individual I am talking about the individual who lives in the collective. To be absolutely honest, that's the only kind of individual there is, for that's the only human there is. Rest are just a mockery of individuality - they are a mockery of humanity.

In the sanctuary of love selfishness is filth. The lover loves themselves by loving the other. The reformer loves themselves by loving the society. The human loves themselves by loving humanity.

Where there is love, there is everything else, everything good that is - equality, inclusion, acceptance, sustainability, everything. But where there is no love, all these fancy terms are mere concepts, they are mere myth, that cannot be made reality even with a thousand policies, think tanks, and humanitarian institutions.

13. Love, Latitude, Longitude
(The Sonnet)

54

Love, Latitude, Longitude
(The Sonnet)

Love knows no latitude,
Love knows no longitude.
Love only knows to be,
Annihilated in servitude.
Love knows no aptitude,
Love knows no sanctitude.
Love only knows to give,
And wind up a destitute.
A destitute lover is wealthier,
Than a loveless billionaire.
Prison of gold is still a prison,
Our own greed makes us prisoner.
Eyes off the gold and hands on the heart!
Thus we shall wipe out all the world's dirt.

14. Ruined Lover (The Sonnet)

58

Ruined Lover
(The Sonnet)

It isn't wrong to want,
To be with someone.
Whether they reciprocate,
Is not your decision.
You cannot force love,
To force love is to ruin it.
All you can do is reach out,
Even at the risk of being ruined.
Love never cares about reputation,
If it did it wouldn't be love.
If you can still think logical,
You are anything but in love.
Logic is but poison in love's domain.
Let all ego be washed away by love's pouring rain.

15. Beyond Recognition

62

One person can revolutionize the universe if there is love in their heart. And self-centricity is the antithesis of a civilized heart. Let me elaborate. Someone asked me the other day, why haven't I won any awards! To which I say - how do you award the Everest! You may designate it as the tallest peak and all that, but how does that make any difference in the greatness of the Everest! Or how do you award the sun and the trees and the birds and the ocean? You simply cannot!

You know why?

Because the greatest forces of good are beyond recognition. They are intertwined with everyday life so very deeply, that people don't think twice, how their life would be if suddenly those forces were to disappear. And that, my friend, is the greatest recognition of all -- the recognition beyond recognition.

You see, once you recognize your humanity, no other recognition holds any appeal. Because in front of the self-fulfilling glory of being human all other glories fall short. Earth's best and bravest must recognize their humanity, only then the world will remember to be human.

Without humanity, all prayer is pestilence, all policy is fallacy, all law is lethargy.

The problem is, in a world of humans the humans focus on everything else but humanity. That's why every single solution we come up with by means of technology and all that, creates its own new set of problems. Hence a society plagued by disease and disparity remains plagued till kingdom come.

We come up with social media to connect the world, and inadvertently shove the world into the death-pit of depression. We come up with cryptocurrency to bypass the coldness and corruption of financial institutions, and inadvertently we end up making way for a tsunami of untraceable fraudulence.

All because we try to fix the troubles of the human society without actually taking humanity into account.

16. No Collaboration With Cancer

If we wipe out humanity from our fancy equations, then we only wipe out ourselves. With such acts of fallacy how can we expect there to be any advancement in the world whatsoever?

Even our very notion of advancement is all messed up. Our notion of advancement prioritizes colonizing Mars over feeding the hungry and sheltering the homeless. If this is advancement, then the pioneers of such advancement are nothing but cancer on the face of earth.

And just like you don't collaborate with Adolf Hitler, you don't collaborate with such pioneers, that is, with toxic billionaires. If you do, then you are no better than those rich and reckless kids of emerald mine owners.

So I say again, the fate of this world lies in the hands of the civilians - everyday, ordinary civilians. When the civilians are responsible, the world is well - when the civilians are sapient, the world is swell.

You may ask, are all billionaires evil?

To which I say, for the sake of decency and pomposity we may naively proclaim that not all billionaires are evil, but the fact of the matter is, in this particular case, that is, when we are talking about billionaires, all billionaires are hypocrites, because if they were not, they wouldn't be billionaires in the first place, for by their own free will they would have utilized their over-abundance of funds to equalize the society.

Remember this, money doesn't fix the world, responsibility does. Responsibility puts a roof over the homeless, responsibility puts food in empty stomachs, responsibility elevates the fallen and forgotten parts of the world.

This is law. This is life.

17. Money Doesn't Fix The World

We've been taught to think that money fixes all the problems of the world. That's why the entire world continues to remain wrecked by unsustainability. Greed of gold may bring green of dollar, but in time it destroys all green of nature and neurons.

So what is the answer?

The answer is responsibility. Once we feel responsible for each other's sorrows, once we feel responsible for each other's happiness, once we feel responsible for each other's uplift, sustainability will rain on all of us like nobody's business.

But mark you, this is not the responsibility of a court judge, but that of a lover - a crazy lover who has lost all sense of self. That's the kind of responsibility that will fix this world, or to be more accurate, that's the kind of responsibility that will humanize this theoretically human world, once it unfolds through civilian behavior.

Each of us is a chunk of uranium, extremely unstable, but extremely potent.

So answer me this - will you utilize that potential or just continue to whine about your instabilities. I know you are unstable – do you know how I know - because I am too - but whether that instability will break you or be a stepping stone in your making, in the making of this world, in the making of civilization, it depends on you, and you alone.

You may come across some who proclaim nothing bothers them.

So let me tell you a secret.

If nothing bothers you, it doesn't mean you are stable, it means you are dead.

18. One Sense Above All

There is no humanity without some instability, because through instability we develop integrity.

So I ask you again, how will you use that potential?

If you use it to chase self-serving interests then you'll only become further unstable and eventually take the world down with you. But if you use your potential to light the world, then your instability will endow this world with real, lasting stability - the kind of stability that's not reliant on revenue - the kind of stability that is not founded on limitless greed and reckless luxury.

So walk past your whining and grow some vagina my friend - grow some vagina.

And no, I have not assumed your gender. Here I am using the term "vagina" as the rightful reference to resilience.

People keep using the term "pu**y" to refer to someone weak. I say, have you ever studied a "pu**y"? Let me tell you something as a biologist and behaviorist. A "pu**y" is ten times stronger and more resilient than any "d**k" in the world.

A vagina can do whatever a penis can do, ten times more efficiently, and that too while bleeding.

Anyway, let's get back to the matter at hand.

Strength is needed, resilience is needed, reason is needed, and all of it is to be guided by a sense of responsibility - human responsibility - the sense that makes one human.

The human body may have five senses, but the human being has only one - accountability.

Apathy and humanity are antithesis of each other. Indifference and humanity are antithesis of each other.

Inert objects look good on the mantelpiece. That's about all. They have no other role under the sun. Don't be a showpiece on the mantelpiece my friend - be a mental piece, and blow your top every time you witness an injustice taking place, and do whatever is necessary to restrain the wrong.

And remember, you don't need status to restrain the wrong – you don't need status to humanize the world, you just need a backbone.

Do you have one?

Then what are you waiting for?

Demolish every last trace of materialism from your life, and stand up as a responsible human being - the kind with backbone.

19. Scrutiny Must Never Cease

Growth requires the acceptance of the most uncomfortable truth. And the truth is that, our world is unsustainable because of all its excessive and rather reckless materialism. In this pathetic world of ours, instead of matter serving the mind, it's the mind that serves matter.

What a pity!

All that potential of the most magnificent and capable organic marvel in the known universe is going to waste!

What a pity!

Why?

Because we don't know the difference between liberty and recklessness.

Because we think liberty means having no line whatsoever.

So let me tell you something.

Liberty doesn't mean having no line, liberty means scrutinizing the existing lines and drawing new ones while abolishing the ones that are no longer relevant with the time.

Scrutiny of traditions and habits must never cease - whether they are old or new.

Our ancestors weren't infallible, we are not infallible, our descendants won't be infallible. Therefore, self-correction must never cease.

And I am not talking about a cold and heartless drive for correction. We need correction, but we need correction with heart. We need correction because we wanna heal, not because we hate.

The nature of our intent makes a great difference in the outcome in the long run.

As a matter of fact, human intent determines human destiny - it determines the fate of an entire species. That is why I say, revolution starts with self-regulation - self-regulation with the intent of health and harmony.

Let me give you an example. You buy a car for transport, not to live at the gas station. Likewise, you earn money to access essentials, not to live at the shopping mall.

There is a life outside the shopping mall. When you understand this, you'll understand sustainability.

So to put it another way, self-regulation is the foundational act behind all sustainability. Regulate yourself and you shall rejuvenate the world. No matter who lives how, you for one live as the walking epitome of sustainability – you for one live as the walking epitome of true human existence.

20. Old and New (The Sonnet)

Old and New
(The Sonnet)

Old is not necessarily gold,
New is not necessarily cool.
Stereotypes without scrutiny,
Sustain only a society of fools.
Answer to one stereotype is not another,
Answer to one assumption is not another.
To make assumption is not wrong but,
To assume it as truth supreme is rhubarb.
Perception is all about assumption,
Our brain hasn't evolved to observe reality.
Biases prevent the observation of biases, unless,
You are hellbent to expand across comfort and luxury.
Stereotypes are archetypes of self-preservation.
Look outside the self and you'll find assimilation.

21. Fortune Without Love
(The Sonnet)

Fortune Without Love
(The Sonnet)

Fortune without love is sheer curse,
For life's true blessing is love alone.
Live to love and love to live,
With this as motto all good is honed.
They say you can't live on love alone,
And indeed it's true to its factual core.
But green of dollar without green of heart,
Grows on us like toxic mold.
Too much of dollar can kill a person,
Just like too little causes starvation.
Use money like you use your car,
To go places, not to live at the gas station.
Put love and life above all else.
You'll know what's sense, what's nonsense.

22. It Won't Be Easy

94

Know this. It won't be easy. If you choose to live as human, and not as a human-looking animal, it won't be easy - the animals of the world will make things extremely difficult for you. But do not move an inch from your conviction - because only then your light will foster the might to cross the threshold of hate, and spark humanity in other possible vessels, low in number though they may be.

Remember this. In a world of animals one who is human has more haters than admirers. And believe you me, this is easier said than felt. And when you have to face it every single day, it is very much possible that sometimes you may end up doubting your own convictions.

But fret not, when a reformer has more haters than admirers it doesn't mean they are on the wrong path, rather it means the opposite, it means you are on the right path. It means your conviction of humanity is acting as bitter antiseptic ointment on inhumanity.

Believe you me, I wish I didn't have to say this. But situation has compelled me. So hear me well. To sustain the world you must sustain yourself across the hate.

Fall, it's okay - just don't fall out of your conviction, don't fall out of your revolution, don't fall out of your love for society. And mark you me, if your love is real, you will never fall out of it.

So I ask you this.

Inhumanity is plenty, torment is plenty. Are you the ointment, or just another senseless sapiens?

But mark you, do not think of this to be a competition. As a matter of fact, competition has no place in a sustainable society.

So what does, if not competition?

Excellence.

23. Sapient or Savage
(The Sonnet)

Sapient or Savage
(The Sonnet)

To be or not to be,
That is not the question.
To be human or stay animal,
That is the question.
Human and animal,
What is the difference!
To be animal is to be selfish,
To be human is to go beyond the self.
There's more to life than us and them,
There's more to life than loss and gain.
There's more to life than money and fame,
There's more to life than dogmatic lanes.
To be or not to be, that is not the question.
Be sapient or stay savage, it's your decision.

24. Life is Chaos (The Sonnet)

Life is Chaos
(The Sonnet)

Best laid plans of mice and men,
Often go awry leaving no hope.
Just when you think you have control,
Life throws you off course.
All notions of order are a myth,
Only order of the universe is chaos.
Expand your sight and you'll realize,
There is order in every chaos.
A narrow mind is ever struggling,
In the tangled web of order and chaos.
A sapient mind works above the two,
For their sight is fixed on a purpose.
Focus on life, not on all its philosophy.
Embrace the chaos and act despite insecurity.

25. Light Impossible
(The Sonnet)

Light Impossible
(The Sonnet)

A candle knows only to give light,
Despite being surrounded by darkness.
Darkness cannot affect the candle's light,
A candle cannot be coerced into heartlessness.
The struggle for light has never been easy,
If it were, light would be but a cigarette-butt.
Light is priceless, hence the struggle is eternal,
To be light is to be alive, even amidst the dark.
To be light is to see light, this is the law,
To be good is to see good, this is the way.
One whose hands are guided by love and light,
Even amidst ominous storms never goes astray.
Love for the world causes light impossible.
For love for the people is love untameable.

26. Competition Breeds Sickness

I have always asked you to place attention on excellence, as opposed to competition. So at a recent event I was asked, how is excellence different from competition? And this is indeed a fair question, for people often assume than the only way to achieve excellence is through competition.

So let's investigate it further.

Competition is the enemy of wellness, which means that competition is the antithesis of sustainability. Competition breeds nothing but sickness.

Let me elaborate.

Competition involves fight for survival, whereas excellence is the struggle for uplift. Excellence involves your desire to grow, but not by dragging somebody else down – or by being superior to somebody.

Competition means you wanna be superior to others, whereas excellence means you wanna be excellent in what you do.

In competition your focus is on diminishing other people, whereas in excellence your focus is not on diminishing other people, rather on elevating your capacities.

In short, excellence is the sharpening of a capacity, competition is the diminishing of other people.

You don't rise by dragging another down. Yet that seems to be the norm in this selfishness peddling world of ours. So you gotta stand your ground firmly with Himalayan strength, against the entire cockeyed world if necessary, for your failure means the failure of humanity. And this no failure in some petty professional task, rather it is the supreme failure of human life.

The world has been failing us since time immemorial, by selling us selfishness, by selling us materialism, by selling us snobbery, by selling us indifference and self-centricity.

It is time we stop failing ourselves - it is time we stop failing the spirit of love and life that lies dormant in us.

You'll face a lot of hate, almost to an unimaginable extent, but do not let hate turn you into another hater. If you do, it's the triumph of hate and defeat of the human – if you do, it is the triumph of inhumanity and defeat of humanity.

27. Hate Not The Hater
(The Sonnet)

Hate Not The Hater
(The Sonnet)

In most cases what seems,
Like hate is actually envy.
Even the haters don't know that,
Haters just hate what they can't be.
Others' achievement intimidates the puny,
Whereas it inspires those wanting to grow.
Pay no attention to the mockery of morons,
Ridicule can't diminish a braveheart's glow.
When an empty flashlight mocks the sun,
Does it affect the sun's glory one bit!
Hate not the haters in return my friend,
It's just their way of acting needy, that's it.
One lover is braver than a hundred haters.
One heart alive and aloud is the bias breaker.

28. Valley of Light
(The Sonnet)

Valley of Light
(The Sonnet)

Behind every cloud,
There is a silver lining.
The cloud is in the mind,
So is the silver lining.
The brush is born of mind,
The paint as well is born of mind.
If the painting has no color,
That too is because of the mind.
When the mind is bright so is the sun,
When the heart is dark so is the sun.
When everything looks dull, just look inside,
You'll discover, all along you've been the sun.
Heart is the gateway to its own valley of light.
Heart is the pedestrian, heart is the might.

29. Be The Precedent

124

Life finds a way when love finds a way, and love finds a way when the human makes a way. So, shall we? Make a way that is.

Together we shall make a way, together we shall make a world.

You know why?

Because togetherness is the way.

And if you think you are alone in building the world, remember this.

I am your precedent. In the same way, keep on doing your duty, so that you may become the precedent for somebody else.

And just like that, each being the precedent to another, each being the residence to another, we shall build the universal residence of love and light for everybody - where nobody will be alien, nobody will be destitute, where nobody will be persecuted, nobody will have reason to be rude.

And no - I am not talking about some fictitious, supernatural utopia. All I am asking is that we humans be human - all I am stating is this.

Be a dawn where there is none, be the air where there is none, be the will where there is none.

You see, there is no supernatural, only natural yet to be understood. And as for various phenomena of the supernatural and paranormal, I'll say it to you plainly.

In all phenomena of the supernatural, it's either nature playing tricks on us, or our own mind playing tricks on us, or another mortal playing tricks on us.

And believe you me, building a world where the human is to behave human and to be treated as such, is anything but supernatural or mythical.

So far nature has determined what's natural, what's not. It is time we take the reins on matters of human behavior, even if it goes against the traditions of nature.

Now the question is, can we really go against nature? We can, because nature herself has engraved the capacity in us to do so, for in nature nothing is hardwired, everything is livewired, everything is evolvable.

30. We Are Nature's Wonder

We are the greatest manifestation of nature's wonder. We are the greatest experiment of mother nature. And here's the most fascinating bit. The fate of this experiment lies, not in the hands of nature, but in the hands of us humans, for all the ingredients needed for the experiment, that is, the biological brain potential, are already endowed to us via natural selection.

Now to the bitter part.

We've been destroying nature ever since we started industrializing. But no worries - nature can sustain herself whether we do anything about it or not. But the point is, once nature starts sustaining herself against our narcissistic deeds, there won't be any trace of us left, no matter how technologically advanced we are.

One thing you must know about science and technology. No science, no technology, is superior to nature. To assume otherwise is to invite doom.

Hence it is more reason for us to focus on sustainability. Therefore it is more reason to give up our ostentatious self-centricity. If we don't, nature will do it to us with a kick in the butt and a stone on our tomb, that says, "the species that brought their own doom".

Climate justice, economic justice, social justice, all these are intertwined with each other. And one single key will unlock them all - the key of simple and accountable living.

So the simple fact of the matter is this. Sustainability is not a fantasy, it's not a pomposity - sustainability is necessity - all of which starts with us being not a bunch of narcissistic morons.

I know we are not used to it, but let's give it a try anyways, because the alternative is extinction.

So, let's be simple, shall we!

Let's be humble, shall we!

Let's be human, shall we!

And for that if they call you a nut, let them.

**31. Peygamber Undercover
(Sonnet of Accountability)**

Peygamber Undercover
(Sonnet of Accountability)

Everywhere I look, there's apocalypse!
Everywhere I look, there's inhumanity!
We have slept like a log long enough!
It's time for the human to embody humanity!
Still if you ask out of fear and insecurity,
What can you one person do to bring change!
Mark my words, if you are really determined,
You could part the ocean with sheer intent.
You have the power to turn this ailing world,
Into a world of laughter and loveliness.
The question is, are you a responsible human,
Or just another crummy vessel of recklessness?
Whatever the trouble may be, you are the answer.
In this difficult time, you are peygamber undercover.

32. Yeni Peygamber
(Sorumluluk Şiiri – Turkish)

Yeni Peygamber*
(Sorumluluk Şiiri)

Her yerde hayvan!
Her yerde kıyamet!
Yeter ceset gibi uyumak!
İnsan insan olmalı, zaman geldi!
Yine de eğer sen bana sorarsan,
Tek başına ne yapabilirsin!
Gerçekten istiyorsan, tek başına,
Dünyaya insanlığı öğretebilirsin.
Eğer istersen, tek başına, insanların,
Ağlamayı gülümsemeye dönüştürebilirsin.
Asıl soru, sen sorumlu bir insan mısın,
Yoksa insan görünümlü bir hayvan mısın?
Uyan kardeşim, her hayvanlığa cevap sensin.
Bu zor zamanda dünyanın yeni peygamber sensin.

*Original Turkish version of the sonnet
Peygamber Undercover (Sonnet of Accountability)

33. Sanity and Insanity

The point is, you gotta be insane to some extent, if you are to treat the prehistoric norms of society. Because a self-absorbed world will always believe that to accept such norms as the way of life is sanity.

Which means that you gotta be insane to change the very definition of sanity in this world.

To put it another way.

Sanity begins with insanity, in the context of our current societal condition that is.

Wanna build a just society! Don't take anything for granted, don't take anything as gospel.

Remember, injustice strikes the moment you start taking human rights for granted. Inhumanity strikes the moment you start taking humanity for granted.

Which means, you oughta guard your humanity with your life - we oughta guard our humanness with our life - we oughta cherish our humanness - relish it, replenish it, with all the care and courage in our veins and nerves.

When we replenish our humanity, equality will be replenished. When we replenish our humanity, inclusion will be replenished. When we replenish our humanity, justice will be replenished. When we replenish our humanity, civilization will be replenished.

It all depends on us not giving in to trivialities at the expense of our humanity. Humanity first and foremost - this time, every time.

But then again, what is humanity?

Because to a bigot stuck in the medieval times, being a white supremacist or a divisionistic nationalist is the definition of humanity. So let me put it in words that even a child could understand.

Humanity means expansion, not exclusion - humanity means inclusion, not insurrection.

34. People Vs Supreme Court
(The Sonnet)

People Vs Supreme Court
(The Sonnet)

When the Supreme Court behaves prehistoric,
Every human must become an activist.
When the gatekeepers of law behave barbarian,
Every civilian must come down to the street.
When people are stripped off their basic rights,
By some bigoted and shortsighted gargoyles.
We the people must take back the reins,
And put the politicians in their rightful place.
We need no guns and grenades, we need no ammo,
Unarmed and unbent we stand against savagery.
Till every woman obtains their right to choice,
None of us will sit quiet in compliant apathy.
Every time the cradle of justice becomes criminal,
It falls upon us civilians to be justice incorruptible.

35. Humanity Means

Humanity means bringing down the walls, not raising more of them. Humanity means demolition of divisions, not the glorification of divisions.

I am compelled to mention this simple thing in so many different ways, you know why? Because bigots keep finding ways to use my work as support for their bigotry and divisionism.

But here's the thing. The fact of the matter is, no matter how much I try, there'll always be some who'll use me as shield for their prejudice, ignorance and narrow-mindedness.

So I'll just say it plain and simple. I don't write for these morons.

My ideas are ammunition in the struggle for equality, my ideas are ingredients of assimilation - they are the spirit of unification. Using my ideas otherwise to fulfill some silly prehistoric tendencies, is like using the sun to spread darkness.

And the intriguing part is, I am not the exclusive source of my ideas. I am the spirit of uplift and assimilation, which means that, anybody working in the course of justice and equality, conquering their petty divisionistic tendencies, is bound to realize the same spirit that I have, whether they have studied me or not.

That's the beauty of the spirit of oneness. I am just a twig, whereas the spirit is universal. The spirit in you is the spirit in me, and all divisions are an illusion.

Feel the spirit, dream the spirit, live the spirit - the spirit of equality, the spirit of reason, the spirit of ascension and assimilation. Once you do, all sustainability will come on its own.

BIBLIOGRAPHY

Archer M., (2000), Being Human: The Problem of Agency. Cambridge University Press.

Adolphs R (2003) Cognitive neuroscience of human social behaviour. Nature Rev Neurosci 4: 165–178.

Adolphs R, Tranel D, Damasio AR (2003) Dissociable neural systems for recognizing emotions. Brain Cogn 52: 61–69.

Andresen, Jensine, and Robert Forman, eds. Cognitive Models and Spiritual Maps. Bowling Green, Ohio: Imprint Academic, 2000.

Azari, Nina, Janpeter Nickel, Gilbert Wunderlich, Michael Niedeggen, Harald Hefter, Lutz Tellmann, Hans Herzog, Petra Stoerig, Dieter Birnbacher, and Rudiger Seitz. "Neural Correlates of Religious Experience."

European Journal of Neuroscience 13, no. 8 (2001)

Agar, N. (2004). Liberal eugenics: In defence of human enhancement. London: Blackwell Publishing.

Alteheld, N., Roessler, G., Vobig, M., & Walter, R. (2004). The retina implant new approach to a visual prosthesis. Biomedizinische Technik, 49(4), 99–103.

Antal, A., Nitsche, M. A., Kincses, T. Z., Kruse, W., Hoffmann, K. P., & Paulus, W. (2004a). Facilitation of visuo-motor learning by transcranial direct current stimulation of the motor and extrastriate visual areas in humans. European Journal of Neuroscience, 19(10), 2888–2892.

Bernstein R.J., (1971), Praxis and Action: Contemporary Philosophies of Human Activity. Philadelphia: University of Pennsylvania Press.

Bernstein R.J., (1976), The Restructuring Social and Political Thought.

Bernstein R.J., (1983), Beyond Relativism and Objectivism: Science, Hermeneutics, and Praxis. Philadelphia: University of Pennsylvania Press.

Bernstein R.J., (1986), Philosophical Profiles. Philadelphia: University of Pennsylvania Press.

Bernstein R.J., (1991), New Constellation. Cambridge: MIT Press.

Birkhead, T. R., Johnson, S. D. & Nettleship, D. N. (1985). Extra-pair matings and mate guarding in the common murre Uria aalge. - Anim. Behav. 33, p. 608-619.

Beauregard, Mario, and Vincent Paquette. "Neural Correlates of a Mystical Experience in Carmelite Nuns." Neuroscience Letters 405, no. 3 (2006)

Benson, Herbert. Timeless Healing: The Power and Biology of Belief. New York: Scribner, 1996

Bose, Subhas Chandra. An Indian Pilgrim: An Unfinished Autobiography, Oxford University Press, 1997

Bogen, J.E.(1995a), 'On the neurophysiology of consciousness: Part I. An overview', Consciousness and Cognition, 4.

Bogen, J.E. (1995b), 'On the neurophysiology of consciousness: Part II. Constraining the semantic problem', Consciousness and Cognition, 4.

Bremner, J. D., R. Soufer, et al. (2001). "Gender differences in cognitive and neural correlates of remembrance of emotional words." Psychopharmacol Bull 35 (3).

Brothers, L. (2002). The social brain: A project for integrating primate behavior and neurophysiology in a new domain. In J. T. Cacioppo et al. (Eds.), Foundations in neuroscience. Cambridge, MA: MIT Press.

Buss, D. D. (2003). Evolutionary Psychology: The New Science of Mind, 2nd ed. New York: Allyn & Bacon.

Buss, D. M. (1989). "Conflict between the sexes: Strategic interference and the evocation of anger and upset." J Pers Soc Psychol 56 (5).

Buss, D. M. (1995). "Psychological sex differences. Origins through sexual selection." Am Psychol 50 (3).

Buss, D. M., and D. P. Schmitt (1993). "Sexual strategies theory: An evolutionary perspective on human mating." Psychol Rev 100 (2).

Blakemore SJ, Decety J (2001) From the perception of action to the understanding of intention. Nature Rev Neurosci 2: 561.

Colapietro V., (1988), "Human Agency: The Habits of Our Being." Southern Journal of Philosophy, XXVI, 2, pp. 153-68.

Colapietro V., (1992), "Purpose, Power, and Agency." The Monist, 75, 4 (October) pp. 423-44.

Colapietro V., (2004a), "C. S. Peirce's Reclamation of Teleology." Nature in American Philosophy, ed. Jean De Groot (Washington, D.C.: Catholic University Press of America), pp. 88-108.

Carey DP, Perrett DI, Oram MW (1997) Recognizing, understanding and reproducing actions. In: Jeannerod M, Grafman J (eds) Handbook of neuropsychology. Vol. 11: Action and cognition. Elsevier, Amsterdam.

Carr L, Iacoboni M, Dubeau MC, Mazziotta JC, Lenzi GL (2003) Neural mechanisms of empathy in humans: a relay from neural systems for imitation to limbic areas. Proc Natl Acad Sci USA 100: 5497–5502.

Chomsky Noam, (2017) Requiem for the American Dream

Chomsky Noam, (2016) Who Rules the World?

Chomsky Noam, (2010) How the World Works

Churchland, P.S. (1986), Neurophilosophy (Cambridge, MA: The MIT Press).

Churchland, P.S. & Ramachandran, V.S. (1993), 'Filling in: Why Dennett is wrong', in Dennett and His Critics: Demystifying Mind, ed. B. Dahlbom (Oxford: Blackwell Scientific Press).

Churchland, P.S., Ramachandran, V.S. & Sejnowski, T.J. (1994), 'A critique of pure vision', in Large- scale Neuronal Theories of the Brain, ed. C. Koch & J.L. Davis (Cambridge, MA: The MIT Press).

Coyle EF. Integration of the physiological factors determining endurance performance ability. Exerc Sport Sci Rev. 1995;23:25–63.

Crick, F. (1994), The Astonishing Hypothesis: The Scientific Search for the Soul (New York: Simon and Schuster).

Crick, F. (1996), 'Visual perception: rivalry and consciousness', Nature, 379.

Crick, F. & Koch, C. (1992), 'The problem of consciousness', Scientific American, 267.

Damasio, A (2003a) Looking for Spinoza. Harcourt Inc. Damasio A (2003b) Feeling of emotion and the self. Ann NY Acad Sci 1001: 253–261.

d'Aquili, Eugene. "Senses of Reality in Science and Religion." Zygon 17, no 4 (1982)

d'Aquili, Eugene. "The Biopsychological Determinants of Religious Ritual Behavior." Zygon 10, no. 1 (1975)

d'Aquili, Eugene. "The Myth-Ritual Complex: A Biogenetic Structural Analysis." Zygon 18, no. 3 (1983)

d'Aquili, Eugene, and Andrew Newberg. The Mystical Mind: Probing the Biology of Religious Experience. Minneapolis: Fortress Press, 1999.

Daly DD. 1958. Ictal affect. Am J Psychiatry.

Damasio, A. (1994) Descartes' Error: Emotion, Reason and the Human Brain. New York, Putnams.

Damasio, A. (1999) The Feeling of What Happens: Body, Emotion and the Making of Consciousness. London, Heinemann.

Darwin, C. (1859) On the Origin of Species by Means of Natural Selection. London, Murray.

Darwin, C. (1871) The Descent of Man and Selection in Relation to Sex. London, John Murray.

Darwin, C. (1872) The Expression of the Emotions in Man and Animals. London, John Murray; also published 1965, Chicago, University of Chicago Press.

Dawkins, M.S. (1987) Minding and mattering. In C. Blakemore and S. Greenfield (eds) Mindwaves. Oxford, Blackwell, 151-60.

Dawkins, R. (1976) The Selfish Gene. Oxford, Oxford University Press; a new edition, with additional material, was published in 1989.

Di Pellegrino G, Fadiga L, Fogassi L, Gallese V, Rizzolatti G (1992) Understanding motor events: A neurophysiological study. Exp Brain Res 91: 176–80.

Deikman, A.J. (2000) A functional approach to mysticism. Journal of Consciousness Studies 7(11-12), 75-91.

Delmonte, M.M. (1987) Personality and meditation. In M. West (ed.) The Psychology of Meditation. Oxford, Clarendon Press, 118-32.

Dennett, D.C. (1988) Quining qualia. In A.J. Marcel and E. Bisiach (eds) Consciousness in Contemporary Science. Oxford, Oxford University Press, 42-77.

Dennett, D.C. (1991) Consciousness Explained. Boston, MA, and London, Little, Brown and Co.

Dennett, D.C. (1995a) Darwin's Dangerous Idea. London, Penguin.

Dennett, D.C. (1998b) Brainchildren: Essays on Designing Minds. Cambridge, MA, MIT Press.

Dewhurst, Kenneth, and A. W. Beard. "Sudden Religious Conversions in Temporal Lobe Epilepsy." British Journal of Psychiatry 117 (1970)

Dewhurst K, Beard AW. Sudden religious conversions in temporal lobe epilepsy. 1970 Epilepsy Behav 2003

Devinsky O, Lai G. Spirituality and religion in epilepsy. Epilepsy Behav 2008.

Devinsky, O., Morrell, MJ, Vogt, BA. (1995) 'Contribution of anterior cingulate cortex to behavior', Brain, 118.

E. Horvitz, "One Hundred Year Study on Artificial Intelligence: Reflections and Framing," ed: Stanford University, 2014.

Eckhart Meister, Selected Writings

Egidi R., ed. (1999), "Von Wright and 'Dante's Dream': Stages in a Philosophical Pilgrim's Progress", in

In Search of a New Humanism: the Philosophy of G.H. von Wright, ed. by R. Egidi, Kluwer, Dordrecht.

Fadiga L, Fogassi L, Pavesi G, Rizzolatti G (1995) Motor facilitation during action observation: a magnetic stimulation study. J Neurophysiol 73: 2608–2611.

Fogassi L, Gallese V, Fadiga L, Rizzolatti G (1998) Neurons responding to the sight of goal directed hand/arm actions in the parietal area PF (7b) of the macaque monkey. Soc Neurosci Abs 24:257.5.

Frith U, Frith CD (2003) Development and neurophysiology of mentalizing. Philos Trans R Soc Lond B Biol Sci 358: 459.

Farah, M.J. (1989), 'The neural basis of mental imagery', Trends in Neurosciences, 10.

Finlay BL, Darlington RB (1995) Linked regularities in the development and evolution of mammalian brains. Science 268.

Freud, S. "The Interpretation of Dreams", 1900

Freud, S. "Selected papers on hysteria and other psychoneuroses" Journal of Nervous and Mental Disease 1909.

Freud, S. "The Origin and Development of Psychoanalysis", 1910

Freud, S. "Psychopathology of everyday life", 1914

Freud, S. "Beyond the Pleasure Principle", 1920

Frith, C.D. & Dolan, R.J. (1997), 'Abnormal beliefs: Delusions and memory', Paper presented at the May, 1997, Harvard Conference on Memory and Belief.

Gay, Volney, ed. Neuroscience and Religion. Plymouth, UK: Lexington Books, 2009.

Gazzaniga, M. S. (1985). The social brain. New York: Basic Books.

Gazzaniga, M.S. (1993), 'Brain mechanisms and conscious experience', Ciba Foundation Symposium, 174.

Geschwind N. "Behavioural changes in temporal lobe epilepsy". Psychol Med. 1979.

Gellhorn, E., Kiely, W.F. "Mystical states of consciousness: neurophysiological and clinical aspects." J Nerv Ment Dis. 1972;154:399-405.

Gilbert SL, Dobyns WB, Lahn BT (2005) Genetic links between brain development and brain evolution. Nat Rev Genet 6.

Gray JA. The Psychology of Fear and Stress. 2nd ed. New York, NY: Cambridge University Press; 1988.

Gloor, P. (1992), 'Amygdala and temporal lobe epilepsy', in The Amygdala: Neurobiological Aspects of Emotion, Memory and Mental Dysfunction, ed J.P. Aggleton (New York: Wiley-Liss).

Greenspan, S. I. and S. G. Shanker (2004). The first idea: How symbols, language, and intelligence evolved from our early primate ancestors to modern humans. Cambridge, MA: Da Capo Press.

Grady, D. (1993), 'The vision thing: Mainly in the brain', Discover, June.

Gallagher HL, Frith CD (2003) Functional imaging of 'theory of mind'. Trends Cogn Sci 7: 77.

Gallese V, Fogassi L, Fadiga L, Rizzolatti G (2002) Action representation and the inferior parietal lobule. In: Prinz W, Hommel B (eds) Attention & Performance XIX. Common mechanisms in perception and action. Oxford University Press, Oxford.

Gallese V, Keysers C, Rizzolatti G (2004) A unifying view of the basis of social cognition. Trends Cogn Sci 8: 396–403.

Goldman AI, Sripada CS (2004) Simulationist models of face-based emotion recognition. Cognition 94: 193–213.

Grèzes J, Costes N, Decety J (1998) Top-down effect of strategy on the perception of human biological motion: a PET investigation. Cogn Neuropsychol 15: 553–582.

Grèzes J, Armony JL, Rowe J, Passingham RE (2003) Activations related to "mirror" and "canonical" neurones in the human brain: an fMRI study. Neuroimage 18: 928–937.

Gross CG, Rocha-Miranda CE, Bender DB (1972) Visual properties of neurons in the inferotemporal cortex of the macaque. J Neurophysiol 35: 96–111.

Guevara Che, The Motorcycle Diaries, 1992

Hari R, Forss N, Avikainen S, Kirveskari S, Salenius S, Rizzolatti G (1998) Activation of human primary motor cortex during action observation: a neuromagnetic study. Proc. Natl Acad Sci USA 95: 15061–15065.

Hardy, G. H. (1940). Ramanujan. Cambridge: Cambridge University Press.

Hall, Daniel, Keith Meador, and Harold Koenig. "Measuring Religiousness in Health Research: Review and Critique." Journal of Religion and Health 47, no. 2 (2008)

Harris, Sam, Jonas Kaplan, Ashley Curiel, Susan Bookheimer, Marco Iacoboni, and Mark Cohen. "The Neural Correlates of Religious and

Nonreligious Belief." PLoS One 4, no. 10 (October 1, 2009)

Halgren, E. (1992), 'Emotional neurophysiology of the amygdala within the context of human cognition', in The Amygdala: Neurobiological Aspects of Emotion, Memory and Mental Dysfunction, ed J.P. Aggleton (New York: Wiley-Liss).

Halligan PW, Fink GR, Marshal JC, Vallar G. 2003. Spatial cognition: evidence from visual neglect. Trends Cogn Sci.

Handbook of Emotions, Edited by Michael Lewis, Jeannette M. Haviland-Jones, and Lisa Feldman Barrett, The Guilford Press; 3rd edition (2010).

Hameroff, S.R. and Penrose, R. (1996) Conscious events as orchestrated space-time selections. Journal of Consciousness Studies 3(1), 36-53; also reprinted in J. Shear (ed.) (1997) Explaining Consciousness-The Hard

Problem. Cambridge, MA, MIT Press, 177-95.

Harding, D.E. (1961) On Having no Head: Zen and the Re-Discovery of the Obvious. London, Buddhist Society.

Hardy, A. (1979) The Spiritual Nature of Man: A Study of Contemporary Religious Experience. Oxford, Clarendon Press.

Harre, R. and Gillett, G. (1994) The Discursive Mind. Thousand Oaks, CA, Sage.

Haugeland, J. (ed.) (1997) Mind Design II: Philosophy, Psychology, Artificial Intelligence. Cambridge, MA, MIT Press.

Hauser, M.D. (2000) Wild Minds: What Animals Really Think. New York, Henry Holt and Co.; London, Penguin.

Hebb, D.O. (1949) The Organization of Behavior. New York, Wiley.

Helmholtz, H.L.F. von (1856-67) Treatise on Physiological Optics.

Hess, EH (1975) "The role of pupil size in communication," Scientific American, 233(5), 110–12.

Heyes, C.M. (1998) Theory of mind in nonhuman primates. Behavioral and Brain Sciences 21, 101-48; with commentaries.

Heyes, C.M. and Galef, B.G. (eds) (1996) Social Learning in Animals: The Roots of Culture. San Diego, CA, Academic Press.

Hilgard, E.R. (1986) Divided Consciousness: Multiple Controls in Human Thought and Action. New York, Wiley.

Hilton, E.N., Lundberg, T.R. Transgender Women in the Female Category of Sport: Perspectives on Testosterone Suppression and Performance Advantage. Sports Med 51, 199–214 (2021).

Hitler, Adolf. Mein Kampf, 1925

Hodgson, R. (1891) A case of double consciousness. Proceedings of the Society for Psychical Research 7, 221-58.

Hofstadter, D.R. and Dennett, D.C. (eds) (1981) The Mind's I: Fantasies and Reflections on Self and Soul. London, Penguin.

Holland, J. (ed.) (2001) Ecstasy: The Complete Guide: A Comprehensive Look at the Risks and Benefits of MDMA. Rochester, VT, Park Street Press.

Holmes, D.S. (1987) The influence of meditation versus rest on physiological arousal. In M. West (ed.) The Psychology of Meditation. Oxford, Clarendon Press, 81-103.

Holmstrom, David. 1992, Christian Science Monitor

Holt, J. (1999) Blindsight in debates about qualia. Journal of Consciousness Studies 6(5), 54-71.

Holloway RL (1996) Evolution of the human brain. In: Lock A, Peters CR (eds) Handbook of human symbolic evolution. Oxford University Press, Oxford

Iacoboni M, Woods RP, Brass M, Bekkering H, Mazziotta JC, Rizzolatti G (1999) Cortical mechanisms of human imitation. Science 286: 2526–2528.

Iacoboni M, Koski LM, Brass M, Bekkering H, Woods RP, Dubeau MC, Mazziotta JC, Rizzolatti G (2001) Reafferent copies of imitated actions in the right superior temporal cortex. Proc Natl Acad Sci USA 98: 13995–13999.

Jeannerod M (1988) The neural and behavioural organization of goal-directed movements. Clarendon Press, Oxford.

Johnson-Frey SH, Maloof FR, Newman-Norlund R, Farrer C, Inati S, Grafton ST (2003) Actions or hand-objects interactions? Human inferior frontal cortex and action observation. Neuron 39: 1053–1058.

Jackson, F. (1982) Epiphenomenal qualia. Philosophical Quarterly 32, 127-36.

James, W. (1890) The Principles of Psychology (2 volumes). London, Macmillan.

James, W. (1902) The Varieties of Religious Experience: A Study in Human Nature. New York and London, Longmans, Green and Co.

Jansen, K. (2001) Ketamine: Dreams and Realities. Sarasota, FL, Multidisciplinary Association for Psychedelic Studies.

Jay, M. (ed.) (1999) Artificial Paradises: A Drugs Reader. London, Penguin.

Jaynes, J. (1976) The Origin of Consciousness in the Breakdown of the Bicameral Mind. New York, Houghton Mifflin.

Johnson, M.K. and Raye, C.L. (1981) Reality monitoring. Psychological Review 88, 67-85.

Kadim I, Mahgoub O, Baqir S et al. (2015) Cultured meat from muscle stem cells: a review of challenges and prospects. J Integr Agr 14: 222–233

Kandel, E. R. In Search of Memory: The Emergence of a New Science of Mind, W. W. Norton & Company (2007).

Kandel E. R. Schwartz JH, Jessel TM. Principles of neural sciences. New York; McGraw Hill, 2000.

Kanwisher, N. (2001) Neural events and perceptual awareness. Cognition

79, 89-113; also reprinted inS. Dehaene (ed.) The Cognitive Neuroscience of Consciousness. Cambridge, MA, MIT Press, 89-113.

Karn, K. and Hayhoe, M. (2000) Memory representations guide targeting eye movements in a natural task. Visual Cognition 7, 673-703.

Kennedy, H., & Dehay, C. (1988). Functional implications of the anatomical organization of the callosal projections of visual areas V1 and V2 in the macaque monkey. Behav. Brain Res., 29, 225–236.

Kentridge, R.W. and Heywood, C.A. (1999) The status of blindsight. Journal of Consciousness Studies 6(5), 3-11.

Kihlstrom, J.F. (1996) Perception without awareness of what is perceived, learning without awareness of what is learned. In M. Velmans (ed.) The Science of Consciousness. London, Routledge, 23-46.

Kosslyn, S.M. (1980) Image and Mind. Cambridge, MA, Harvard University Press.

Kosslyn, S.M. (1988) Aspects of a cognitive neuroscience of mental imagery. Science 240, 1621-6.

Kinsbourne, M. (1995), 'The intralaminar thalamic nucleii', Consciousness and Cognition, 4.

Kjaer, Troels, Camilla Bertelsen, Paola Piccini, David Brooks, Jorgen Alving, and Hans Lou. "Increased Dopamine Tone during Meditation- Induced Change of Consciousness." Cognitive Brain Research 13, no. 2 (April 2002)

Kölmel HW. 1985. Complex visual hallucinations in the hemianopic field. J Neurol Neurosurg Psychiatry.

Koenig, Harold. "Research on Religion, Spirituality, and Mental Health: A Review." Canadian Journal of Psychiatry 54, no. 5 (May 2009)

Koenig, Harold, ed. Handbook of Religion and Mental Health. San Diego, CA: Academic Press, 1998

Kraepelin E. Psychiatry: A Textbook for Students and Physicians. New York, NY: Science History Publications; 1990.

Lauglin, Charles, John McManus, and Eugene d'Aquili. Brain, Symbol, and Experience. 2nd ed. New York: Columbia University Press, 1992

Lakoff, G. and M. Johnson (1999). Philosophy in the flesh. Basic Books: New York.

LeDoux, J. E. (1996). The emotional brain. New York: Simon & Schuster.

LeDoux, J.E. (1992), 'Emotion and the amygdala', in The Amygdala: Neurobiological Aspects of Emo- tion, Memory and Mental Dysfunction, ed J.P. Aggleton (New York: Wiley-Liss).

Levin, D.T. and Simons, D.J. (1997) Failure to detect changes to attended objects in motion pictures. Psychonomic Bulletin and Review 4, 501-6.

Levine,J. (1983) Materialism and qualia: the explanatory gap. Pacific Philosophical Quarterly 64, 354-61.

Levine,J. (2001) Purple Haze: The Puzzle of Consciousness. New York, Oxford University Press. Levine, S. (1979) A Gradual Awakening. New York, Doubleday.

Levinson, B.W. (1965) States of awareness during general anaesthesia. British Journal of Anaesthesia 37, 544-6.

Lewicki, P., Czyzewska, M. and Hoffman, H. (1987) Unconscious acquisition of complex procedural knowledge. Journal of Experimental Psychology: Learning, Memory and Cognition 13, 523-30.

Lewicki, P., Hill, T. and Bizot, E. (1988) Acquisition of procedural knowledge about a pattern of stimuli that cannot be articulated. Cognitive Psychology 20, 24-37.

Lewicki, P., Hill, T. and Czyzewska, M. (1992) Nonconscious acquisition of information. American Psychologist 47, 796-801.

Manthey S, Schubotz RI, von Cramon DY (2003). Premotor cortex in observing erroneous action: an fMRI study. Brain Res Cogn Brain Res 15: 296–307.

Mesulam MM, Mufson EJ (1982) Insula of the old world monkey. III: Efferent cortical output and comments on function. J Comp Neurol 212: 38–52.

Naskar, Abhijit. "Homo: A Brief History of Consciousness", 2015

Naskar, Abhijit. "What is Mind?", 2016

Naskar, Abhijit. "Love, God & Neurons: Memoir of A Scientist who found himself by getting lost", 2016

Naskar, Abhijit. "Principia Humanitas", 2017

Naskar, Abhijit. "We Are All Black: A Treatise on Racism", 2017

Naskar, Abhijit. "Either Civilized or Phobic: A Treatise on Homosexuality", 2017

Naskar, Abhijit. "The Bengal Tigress: A Treatise on Gender Equality", 2017

Naskar, Abhijit. "Morality Absolute", 2017

Naskar, Abhijit. "Build Bridges not Walls: In the name of Americana", 2018

Naskar, Abhijit. "Fabric of Humanity", 2018

Naskar, Abhijit. "Citizens of Peace: Beyond the Savagery of Sovereignty", 2019

Naskar, Abhijit. "The Constitution of The United Peoples of Earth", 2019

Naskar, Abhijit. "Neurons Giveth, Neurons Taketh Away | Abhijit Naskar | TEDxIIMRanchi", 2019 https://www.youtube.com/watch?v=BNX-Q0ySm80

Naskar, Abhijit. "Mission Reality", 2019

Naskar, Abhijit. "Operation Justice: To Make A Society That Needs No Law", 2019

Naskar, Abhijit. "Every Generation Needs Caretakers: The Gospel of Patriotism", 2020

Naskar, Abhijit. "Hurricane Humans: Give me accountability, I'll give you peace", 2020

Naskar, Abhijit. "Revolution Indomable", 2020

Naskar, Abhijit. "Servitude is Sanctitude", 2020

Naskar, Abhijit. "Good Scientist: When Science and Service Combine", 2020

Newberg, Andrew, and Jeremy Iversen. "The Neural Basis of the Complex Mental Task of Meditation: Neurotransmitter and Neurochemical Considerations." Medical Hypotheses 61, no. 2 (2003).

Newberg, Andrew. "How God Changes Your Brain: An Introduction to Jewish Neurotheology", CCAR Journal: The Reform Jewish Quarterly, Winter 2016.

Newberg, Andrew, and Stephanie Newberg. "A Neuropsychological Perspective on Spiritual Development." In Handbook of Spiritual Development in Childhood and Adolescence, edited by Eugene

Roehlkepartain, Pamela King, Linda Wagener, and Peter Benson. London: Sage Publications, Inc., 2005

Newberg, Andrew. "The Neurotheology Link An Intersection Between Spirituality and Health", Alternative and Complimentary Therapies, Vol 21 No 1, February 2015.

Newberg, Andrew, Nancy Wintering, Dharma Khalsa, Hannah Roggenkamp, and Mark Waldman. "Meditation Effects on Cognitive Function and Cerebral Blood Flow in Subjects with Memory Loss: A Preliminary Study." Journal of Alzheimer's Disease 20, no. 2 (2010)

Nash, M. (1995), 'Glimpses of the mind', Time.

Nesse RM. Proximate and evolutionary studies of anxiety, stress and depression: synergy at the interface. Neurosci Biobehav Rev. 1999;23:895-903.

Nicolelis, Miguel. (2011) "Beyond Boundaries: The New Neuroscience of Connecting Brains with Machines---and How It Will Change Our Lives", Times Books

O'Hara, K. and Scutt, T. (1996) There is no hard problem of consciousness. Journal of Consciousness Studies 3(4), 290-302, reprinted in J. Shear (ed.) (1997) Explaining Consciousness. Cambridge, MA, MIT Press, 69-82.

O'Regan, J.K. (1992) Solving the "real" mysteries of visual perception: the world as an outside memory. Canadian Journal of Psychology 46, 461-88.

O'Regan, J.K. and Noe, A. (2001) A sensorimotor account of vision and visual consciousness. Behavioral and Brain Sciences 24(5), 883-917.

O'Regan, J.K., Rensink, R.A. and Clark,].]. (1999) Change-blindness as a result of "mudsplashes." Nature 398, 34.

Ornstein, R.E. (1977) The Psychology of Consciousness (2nd edn). New York, Harcourt.

Ornstein, R.E. (1986) The Psychology of Consciousness (3rd edn). New York, Pehguin.

Ornstein, R.E. (1992) The Evolution of Consciousness. New York, Touchstone.

Penfield W, Faulk ME (1955) The insula: further observations on its function. Brain 78: 445– 470.

Penrose, R. (1994), Shadows of the Mind (Oxford: Oxford University Press).

Penrose, R. (1989), The Emperor's New Mind: Concerning Computers, Minds and The Laws of Physics (Oxford: Oxford University Press).

Persinger, "'I would kill in God's name' role of sex, weekly church attendance, report of a religious experience and limbic lability" Perceptual and Motor Skills 1997.

Persinger "Experimental simulation of the God experience" Neurotheology 2003.

Persinger, Corradini, Clement, Keaney, et al "Neurotheology and its convergence with neuroquantology" NeuroQuantology 2010.

Persinger, Koren and St-Pierre "The electromagnetic induction of mystical and altered states within the laboratory" Journal of Consciousness Exploration and Research 2010.

Persinger "Case report: A prototypical spontaneous 'sensed presence' of a sentient being and concomitant electroencephalographic activity in the clinical laboratory" Neurocase 2008.

Persinger and Saroka "Potential production of Hughlings Jackson's "parasitic consciousness" by physiologically-patterned weak transcerebral magnetic fields: QEEG and source localization" Epilepsy & Behavior 28 (2013).

Persinger. "The neuropsychiatry of paranormal experiences". J Neuropsychiatry Clin Neurosci 2001.

Persinger. "Neuropsychological bases of god beliefs", New York: Praeger, 1987

Persinger. "Temporal lobe epileptic signs and correlative behaviors displayed by normal populations", Journal of General Psychology, 1986

Perry BD, Pollard R. Homeostasis, stress, trauma, and adaptation. A neurodevelopmental view of childhood trauma. Child Adolesc Psychiatr Clin N Am. 1998;7:33.

Paré, D. & Llinás, R. (1995), 'Conscious and preconscious processes as seen from the standpoint of sleep-waking cycle neurophysiology', Neuropsychologia, 33.

Phillips ML, Young AW, Senior C, Brammer M, Andrew C, Calder AJ, Bullmore ET, Perrett DI, Rowland D, Williams SC, Gray JA, David AS (1997) A specific neural substrate for perceiving facial expressions of disgust. Nature 389: 495–498.

Phillips ML, Young AW, Scott SK, Calder AJ, Andrew C, Giampietro V, Williams SC, Bullmore ET, Brammer M, Gray JA (1998) Neural responses to facial and vocal expressions of fear and disgust. Proc R Soc Lond B Biol Sci 265: 1809–1817.

Puce A, Perrett D (2003) Electrophysiological and brain imaging of biological motion. Philosoph Trans Royal Soc Lond, Series B, 358: 435–445.

Ramachandran VS. Behavioral and magnetoencephalographic correlates of plasticity in the adult human brain. Proc Natl Acad Sci USA 1993; 90: 10413–20.

Ramachandran VS. Phantom limbs, neglect syndromes, repressed memories, and Freudian psychology. Int Rev Neurobiol 1994; 37: 291–333.

Ramachandran VS. Plasticity and functional recovery in neurology. Clin Med 2005; 5: 368–73.

Ramachandran VS, Hirstein W. The perception of phantom limbs. The D. O. Hebb lecture. Brain 1998; 121: 1603–30.

Ramachandran VS, Rogers-Ramachandran D, Cobb S. Touching the phantom limb. Nature 1995; 377: 489–90.

Ramachandran VS, Rogers-Ramachandran D. Phantom limbs and

neural plasticity. Arch Neurol 2000; 57: 317–20.

Ramachandran VS, Rogers-Ramachandran D. It's all done with mirrors. Sci Am Mind 2007; 18: 16–9.

Ramachandran VS, Rogers-Ramachandran D. Sensations referred to a patient's phantom arm from another subjects intact arm: perceptual correlates of mirror neurons. Med Hypotheses 2008; 70: 1233–4.

Ramachandran VS, Rogers-Ramachandran D, Stewart M. Perceptual correlates of massive cortical reorganization. Science 1992; 258: 1159–60.

Rizzolatti G, Craighero L (2004) The mirror-neuron system. Annu Rev Neurosci 27: 169–192.

Rizzolatti G, Fogassi L, Gallese V (2001) Neurophysiological mechanisms underlying the understanding and imitation of action. Nature Rev Neurosci 2:661–670.

Rock I, Victor J. Vision and touch: an experimentally created conflict between the two senses. Science 1964; 143: 594–6.

Rose´n B, Lundborg G. Training with a mirror in rehabilitation of the hand. Scand J Plast Reconstr Surg Hand Surg 2005; 39: 104–8.

Roberts, TA; Smalley, J; Ahrendt, D (December 2020). "Effect of gender affirming hormones on athletic performance in transwomen and transmen: implications for sporting organisations and legislators". British Journal of Sports Medicine. 55 (11): 577–583

Royet JP, Plailly J, Delon-Martin C, Kareken DA, Segebarth C (2003) fMRI of emotional responses to odors: influence of hedonic valence and judgment, handedness, and gender. Neuroimage 20: 713–728.

Rozin R Haidt J and McCauley CR (2000) Disgust. In: Lewis M, Haviland-Jones JM (eds) Handbook of Emotion. 2nd Edition. Guilford Press, New York, pp 637–653.

Saxe R, Carey S, Kanwisher N (2004) Understanding other minds: linking developmental psychology and functional neuroimaging. Annu Rev Psychol 55: 87–124.

S. J. Russell and P. Norvig, Artificial intelligence: a modern approach (3rd edition): Prentice Hall, 2009.

Singer T, Seymour B, O'Doherty J, Kaube H, Dolan RJ, Frith CD (2004) Empathy for pain involves the affective but not the sensory components of pain. Science 303: 1157–1162.

Smith A (1759) The theory of moral sentiments (ed. 1976). Clarendon Press, Oxford.

Schilling, Vincent. 2017, indian country today

Stein, Stephen K. 2017, The Sea in World History: Exploration, Travel, and Trade

Simonsen R (2015) Eating for the future: veganism and the challenge of in vitro meat. In: Stapleton P, Byers A (Hg). Biopolitics and utopia. Palgrave Macmillan, New York (2015), S 167–190

Tesla N. "My Inventions", 1919

T. R. Society, "Machine learning: the power and promise of computers that learn by example," ed. The Royal Society, 2017.

Tomasello M, Call J (1997) Primate cognition. Oxford University Press, Oxford.

197